C000081645

CHAPTER 3
Deciding on Your Dream

"In order to make your dreams come into reality, it takes
an awful lot of determination, dedication, self-discipline
and effort."

—Jesse Owens[15]

To decide means to determine an outcome, or cut off any
alternate route or path of retreat. To reach your Promised Land and achieve your lifelong dreams, you need to make a
commitment to cut off anything that will keep you from moving
confidently and consistently in that direction. Remember Penny
Chenery's decision that she was not going to sell her horse, Secretariat, to pay off her family's debt? She was so deeply committed
to her dream of making him the greatest racehorse that ever lived
that she refused under any circumstances to surrender to financial
anxiety: "This is about life being ahead of you and you run at it!
Because you never know how far you can run unless you run."[16]

Penny's strong belief in Secretariat's destiny, and her decision
not to sell him, changed my life the night I watched that movie.
It caused me to *decide* to pursue my dream and move to Kentucky. I decided nothing was going to stop me from advancing
towards the life I had always wanted. Doors opened, and I saw
the principles I had studied prove themselves over and over. I
am living proof that when someone commits to their dreams,
all things are possible. In one of his famous articles, Bob Proctor
describes the power of decision:

There is a single mental move you can make which, in a millisecond, will solve enormous problems for you. It has the potential to improve almost any personal or business situation you will ever encounter, and it could literally propel you down the path to incredible success. We have a name for this magic mental activity ... it is called DECISION.[17]

Moses made a decision to obey God in spite of his doubts and fears. When he thrust his staff into the Red Sea, the raging waves parted and allowed the Israelites to advance toward a life of freedom. You, too, must DECIDE to advance boldly toward your own Promised Land. Remember Henry David Thoreau's words: "If one advances *confidently* in the direction of his dreams, and endeavors to live the life which he has imagined, he will meet with a success unexpected in common hours."[18]

The Power of Paradigms

Once you make the decision to boldly step out, your old condition-based thinking and paradigms will begin to show up, just like they did for the Israelites. This is normal. Bob Proctor explains perfectly what paradigms are, and how they influence our daily lives: "A paradigm is a collection of beliefs that are held by a group of people. It's not just one belief held by one person. These beliefs are shared, passed on and believed by generations."[19]

In other words, paradigms are formed through repetition, and over time they manifest in generational beliefs. This is why we see false paradigms being passed on and persisting in families and other groups, and even in whole cultures. The good news is that in taking the step of reading this book, you have shown that you are ready to step out courageously and confront your own false paradigms. This will allow you to overcome negative patterns of behavior carried over from the past, so you can begin operating in a higher order of thinking—what life-transformational teachers call your "genius."

Research has shown that most human beings operate in a much higher percentage of their genius up until around age five. During those first formative years of life, we rely mostly on our intuitive self to learn about the world around us. This natural reliance on intuition starts to decline around the age of five, and by the age of nineteen, most of us operate at about ten percent of our full potential. So what happens around age five that causes us to stop operating in that higher level of genius? What happens is we become conscious of the world around us and the opinions of others.

We then start to doubt ourselves and take on internal judgments passed on from our parents, which they receive from their parents, and so forth. School, our peers, and other external influences such as news, social media, entertainment, and even advertising begin to influence our self-image. The sad outcome of this is that we develop negative, even harsh self-judgments resulting in a sense that WE ARE NOT ENOUGH. This in turn influences our beliefs in who we are and what is possible for us. These false beliefs become deeply rooted in our subconscious and become habitual and are expressed in our personalities.

The reason I am sharing all this with you is not to blame you or previous generations that have influenced your circumstances and decisions. Rather, it's to make you aware of any false paradigms you have operated in that have negatively influenced your decision-making. George Bernard Shaw brilliantly described the problem we run into when we blame outside influences for our conditions:

> People are always blaming their circumstances for what they are. I don't believe in circumstances. The people who get on in this world are the people who get up and look for the circumstances they want and if they can't find them, they make them.[20]

Going forward, it's crucial that you adopt the mindset that YOU ARE FAR GREATER THAN YOUR CIRCUMSTANCES!

Here, again, the Israelites are a great example of how our paradigms can tempt us to blame our circumstances and give up and return to old ways of thinking and behaving. God performed great miracles, liberating them from the captivity of Egypt through the Passover and leading them through roaring waters to freedom. Yet, on their journey when things got tough, what did they do? They complained about their circumstances and even thought they'd be better off retreating back to Egypt! The reason for this response to hardship was that after 400 years of captivity, they had become deeply conditioned to see themselves as slaves. Their entire identity as a culture was so solidified around this idea that they did what we often do when we find ourselves in new territory and facing obstacles—we experience a strong pull to go back to what is familiar, our "comfort zone," even if it is not good for us.

The Power of Words

Another thing that can really hold us back from moving confidently forward is our brokenness from words spoken over us in the past. Words actually have the power to cripple us and prevent us from fulfilling our life's purpose. Les Brown, a well-known motivational speaker and teacher that I greatly admire, tells a powerful story:

> There is one particular person that all of us knew and everybody used to pick at him when he came by. We called him Chicken Man. He had a feather in his hat and a toy chicken on top of his car. He would drive around the downtown area, blinking his lights and occasionally blowing his horn. When he got out of his car he would walk around with a baby carriage, with two baby dolls and a picture of a woman.
>
> When you would say something to him or came near him you would hear him making the sounds of a chicken. All of

Your New Beginning

us used to laugh at Chicken Man. We didn't know Chicken Man's story. Chicken Man woke up one morning around 3 a.m., and his house was on fire. He panicked and got out of the window and left quickly, only to hear his children and wife screaming for help. He ran back to the doorway to save them and the flames were too hot, too awesome. He tried to get in and he couldn't get in. He was desperate and frantic. Pretty soon the cries stopped and they perished in the fire. His brother-in-law came and found out that his sister had died and his nieces in the fire. He grabbed Chicken Man and started to beat him. "You chicken, why didn't you save my sister? YOU'RE A CHICKEN! YOU'RE A CHICKEN!" When the people pulled him off Chicken Man, they said, "Are you alright?" and Chicken Man looked at them and he started making the sounds of a chicken. He never overcame that tragedy. He was stuck from that experience.[21]

This story pierced my heart. We all have life experiences that have affected us like Chicken Man, that have caused us to live a life that is less than what was intended for us. Chicken Man was imprisoned by his circumstances. Words spoken over him by someone whose opinion mattered were so damaging that they altered his perception of who he was. This caused him to condemn himself, to believe that there was no forgiveness for a tragic mistake anyone could make.

The graphic on the next page is a great illustration of how negative feelings founded in our past can overwhelm us sometimes and drown out the truth that we are God's highest form of creation and have tremendous value.

We've all done this to ourselves. The majority of the world is operating under the perception that they are not enough and that their future is defined by their history, and who others say they are. To some degree, all of us are operating under such condition-based thinking and it hinders us from creating a truly abundant life. It's critical that we become aware of thoughts that need changing, in order to gain ground and make progress on our Promised Land journey.

Action Step: Reclaiming Your Worth

What's one wrong message that you have received which made you feel devalued or unworthy, and that you still carry today? Write your thoughts in your notebook. Next, write some new affirmations you can speak over yourself to replace those old, negative messages, so you can now live from a new perspective with a positive identity. I encourage you to use this as your first new affirmation: "I am far greater than any circumstance or situation in my life."

> Children, you belong to God, and you have defeated these enemies. God's Spirit is in you and is more powerful than the one who is in the world.
>
> 1 John 4:4

Stand on this truth until it becomes deeply rooted within you!

The Importance of Self-image

Successful plastic surgeon and author of *Psycho-Cybernetics* Max Maltz had a very keen understanding of how one's perspective affects achievement: "The self-image sets the boundaries of individual accomplishment."[22]

What Maltz is saying here is that your self-image will either empower or limit what you can achieve in this life. So, it's important that you replace false messages you have carried with you, with affirmations reflecting the truth of who God says you are. Remember, you are His highest form of creation and made in His likeness! Your affirmations will become a powerful tool on your daily journey to your Promised Land. I was fortunate to have a mother who spoke positive affirmations over me. I was born on the first day of spring, and every birthday she would say to me, "Happy birthday to my spring baby, he's all about new beginnings!"

The positive message spoken over me in my early years was so powerful and influenced my subconscious so deeply that I formed a belief early on that new beginnings were possible for me and others. This message became very real to me later in life through my faith in Christ and learning about his gift of redemption to humanity.

Sharing this good news became my life's purpose, driven by my passion to share the knowledge that a new beginning is possible for everyone. My hope is that you can find healing through God's grace and replace any negative perceptions of your worth with powerful new affirmations.

I praise You for I am fearfully and wonderfully made.

Psalm 139:14 (ESV)

Speaking positive affirmations may feel foreign at first because from a very young age you may have received false, negative messages that became deeply rooted within you. But, just as false words spoken over you in the past had the power to affect your self-image negatively, you have the power today to speak truth over yourself and transform your life! Even though not everyone received the kind of messages that I did from my mother, it's never too late to start speaking them over yourself today! One of the most effective ways you can counter negative internal messaging is by implementing new affirmations today, through a process called autosuggestion.

Autosuggestion: A Powerful Tool

In his great book *Think and Grow Rich*, Napoleon Hill talks about the power of autosuggestion:

> Autosuggestion is self-suggestion. It is the agency of communication between the part of the mind where conscious thought takes place, and that which serves as the seat of action for the subconscious mind. Through the dominating thoughts which one permits to remain in the conscious mind, (whether these thoughts be negative or positive, is immaterial), the principle of autosuggestion voluntarily reaches the subconscious mind and influences it with these thoughts.

> Nature has so built man that he has ABSOLUTE CONTROL over the material which reaches his subconscious mind through his five senses, although this is not meant to

be construed as a statement that man always EXERCISES this control.[23]

Understanding the power of auto-suggestion, we can implement new ways of speaking truth over ourselves, and start creating new paradigms in line with our true identity. When Andrew Carnegie tasked Napoleon Hill with interviewing 500 of the wealthiest people in the world, he assigned an exercise:

> So I'm going to give you a statement and I want you to repeat this statement to yourself, looking in the mirror every morning and every night. I'm going to give it to you and I want you to write it down. I want you to underline each word, Napoleon.
>
> "This is what I want you to write: Andrew Carnegie, I'm not only going to equal your achievements in life, but I'm going to challenge you at the post and pass you at the grandstand.
>
> Hill threw the pencil on the floor and he said, "Now you know darn well that can't happen!"
>
> "I know it won't happen unless or until you fix that idea in your mind. Now, Napoleon, I want you to make a commitment to me that you will read the statement every morning and every night for 30 days. You can do anything for 30 days," replied Carnegie.
>
> "Yes, I can do that."[24]

Well, you can imagine Hill just whispered the statement to himself the first time. But by the middle of the month, he started to actually believe that he could do it, and by the end of the month, he knew he could do it. And guess what, he did! It has been reported that Carnegie created fifty-three millionaires, but Napoleon Hill has created millions of millionaires. This shows the transformative power of affirmations, no matter what stage we are at in our life's journey.

It's important that you take five minutes at the beginning and end of each day to read your new affirmations *out loud*. Bring your imagination and passion to this exercise. Remember, in this exercise you are already this new person with a healthy and positive self-image. I actually practice speaking affirmations over myself daily, and it continues to change my perspective on who I truly am as a child of the Creator of the universe. Every day, we can choose blessing or cursing with words we speak, including those that we speak over ourselves. The more you speak affirmations into your life, the more you will be able to internalize and believe them and begin to act accordingly.

Let's look again at the graphic from a few pages back, this time with words of affirmation replacing the negative messages of the past. Notice how doing this can shift our entire perspective as we continue to move forward in our Promised Land journey:

CHAPTER 4
Fear and Doubt: The Ten vs. The Two

"Fear is simply the border of the reality you have known,
and your dream is the life that lives beyond that border."[25]

—Mary Morrissey

In this chapter, we are going to cover the subjects of fear and doubt, because just like the Israelites, you're going to experience both of these on your journey to the Promised Land. How you manage them will determine whether or not they become stumbling blocks in your path or steppingstones to a larger faith. When the Israelites finally arrived at Mount Nebo and looked out over the land they had journeyed forty years to reach, they were still struggling to believe that a new beginning was possible. As Numbers 13:2 tells us, God told Moses, "Send men to scout out the country of Canaan that I am giving to the People of Israel. Send one man from each ancestral tribe." But when the ten scouts returned after forty days, they were still captive to fear. This was in spite of the fact that they held in their hands physical evidence that the land really was flowing with milk and honey! Nevertheless, fear and doubt continued to influence their perspective: "But the people who live there are powerful, and the cities are fortified and very large" (Numbers 13:28).

Even when the Promised Land was finally within their sight, fear and doubt caused the ten men to perceive themselves as grasshoppers facing giants! Price Pritchett, author of one of today's most influential life-transformation books, *you*², addresses the mindset of doubt in his chapter "Suspend Disbelief:" "Your doubts are not the product of accurate thinking, but habitual thinking. Years ago you accepted flawed conclusions as correct, and began to live your life as if those warped ideas about your potential were true."[26]

Unlike Joshua and Caleb, the ten tribal leaders succumbed to habitual fear and doubt rooted in flawed generational thinking, and they demonstrated it through their entire wilderness experience. We are all subject at times to the same inaccurate thinking, and we reach false conclusions about what's possible based on our circumstances.

Action step: From Fear to Faith

In your notebook, write down one fear that has been a stumbling block that caused you to doubt what's really possible. In this chapter, you will learn how to shift your perspective on fear so that it actually becomes a steppingstone to a larger faith.

"If you must doubt something, doubt your limits."[27]

—Price Pritchett

I am sure Joshua and Caleb experienced fear at times, too. But, they shifted their attention away from their circumstances and onto the promise that they would inherit the land. This prevented them from even entertaining the doubts that plagued the other ten men. *This is key*: It is one thing to experience fear, but if we *entertain* it, or make it the object of our focus, we give it the power to overtake us. When we shift our focus away from our circumstances onto our Promised Land vision, giant Canaanites and city walls are not threats to be feared, but challenges to overcome on the way to our destination. Why was the perspective of the two, Joshua and Caleb, so different from that of the other men? Because the ten men gave all of their attention to their circumstances, rather than to the promise God had given them. In contrast, Joshua and Caleb's mindset treated the fulfillment of that promise *as a current reality*. This allowed them to suspend disbelief, put fear aside, and move boldly toward their Promised Land vision. They focused on inheriting the land as inevitable! Like Price Pritchett said: "Just act like you have complete faith. Merely do what you'd do if you knew you were going to succeed."[28]

As you advance toward your Promised Land, you must put fear in its place daily so you can begin thinking and acting as if you have already succeeded.

The Nazarene

Jesus of Nazareth is an even more powerful example than Joshua and Caleb of putting fear in its place. My mentor Mary Morrissey described Him as "the perfect template to overcome fear."[29] This description opened my eyes to a whole new way of perceiving and managing my own fear. When Jesus was arguing in the wilderness with Satan (FEAR), His response was the perfect one: "Get behind me."[30] This is always His response to fear, as we see in the story of Peter walking on the water. In the midst of a violent storm on the Sea of Galilee, Peter briefly puts his fear aside and takes a step of faith:

> Jumping out of the boat, Peter walked on the water to Jesus. But when he looked down at the waves churning beneath his feet, he lost his nerve and started to sink. He cried, "Master, save me!" Jesus didn't hesitate. He reached down and grabbed his hand. Then he said, "Faint-heart, what got into you?" The two of them climbed into the boat, and the wind died down.[31] (Matthew 14:29-31)

Peter was momentarily able to suspend disbelief. For just that brief moment, he ignored the waves of doubt and courageously stepped out of the safety of the boat and walked on water. It was when he took his eyes off of Jesus and looked down at the raging sea that he sank. This is something we all do—we take our eyes off of the source of our strength and become submerged in our problems. It's imperative that you step out in faith like Peter did and remain focused on Jesus so you can keep moving forward. This will keep fear from interrupting your progress: "I sought the LORD, and He heard me, and delivered me from all my fears"[32] (Psalm 34:4).

I have had experience putting fear in its place. I recently had the opportunity to train a young, spirited horse named Abraham. I was able to train him to pull a cart in a safe fenced-in arena, but fear that I would lose control and that he would run away kept me from venturing out into the open field. Every day, I would make the excuse that he needed another day of training in the ring. But as a life coach who had learned the principles of managing fear, I knew I had to shift my perspective if I was ever to move beyond the safety of that boundary. I had to trust that with any problem that arose, experience and instinct would kick in and I would know what to do. The day came that I decided I was finally going to venture out of the ring and drive Abraham in the field. That morning, while I was brushing him, I experienced the familiar, sinking feeling of fear in the pit of my stomach. I knew I had to overcome that feeling, so I kept repeating to myself, I have to put this behind me.

I hooked him up to the cart, jumped in, and drove him directly to the field. With that one act, I conquered fear, and I was in my element. The drive was successful and I felt liberated, which gave me the confidence from then on to daily drive him in the freedom of the open field. By kicking aside the stumbling block of fear, I achieved an important step toward the dream I still have that someday I will successfully train and compete with my own horse at the Kentucky State Fair. To get where you want to go, you too must kick the stumbling blocks of fear and doubt aside, and start envisioning yourself living the life you aspire to as a current reality. Using Jesus as your template, you will put fear and doubt in their proper place—which is behind you. This allows you to manage your perception of your circumstances and keep moving forward in your journey. Like Joshua, Caleb, and Peter, this will release you from the captivity of fear and doubt to pursue a life of freedom!

> You have not given me into the hands of the enemy [FEAR] but have set my feet in a spacious place [FREEDOM].[33]
>
> Psalm 31:8 (author's brackets)

Action Step: A Brave Step

What is one brave step you can take today to overcome fear and begin to advance confidently toward your Promised Land?

> "Fear is being scared to death but saddling up anyway."[34]
>
> —John Wayne

Gratitude: The Antidote to Fear of Lack

> "When you are grateful, fear disappears, and abundance appears."[35]
>
> —Tony Robbins

To some extent, all of us operate under a fear of lack. Whether it's lack of money, time, food, or love, we have been conditioned by our life experiences and the constant broadcasts of the world to believe that there is never enough, and that we must compete for resources or do without. This fear leads us to be less generous than we would be if we understood that the universe is abundant and has everything we need to achieve our dreams. Our Creator's nature is one of abundance and generosity. Because we are made in His image, we can be assured that this is our natural state as well. Unfortunately, the fear of lack often prevents us from operating in this truth.

> The life-transformational movement teaches an important concept called the "Law of Circulation," which says that by being generous, we open the doors to abundance in our lives. This universal law is spelled out clearly in Proverbs

11:25 (NLT): "The generous will prosper; those who refresh others will themselves be refreshed."

I'll be honest with you: I have not always operated in generosity. For most of my adult life I've been "horse poor." Sustaining a horse farm is costly, but it has always been my dream. I worked hard at numerous jobs, and most of what I made went to the upkeep of my farms. I had a skewed perception that there was only so much money I could ever make, so my dream always seemed bigger than my paychecks.

In 2008, I became a realtor, and the housing market crashed shortly thereafter, amplifying my fear of lack. Anxiety began to consume me; so much so that I would wake up in the middle of the night in a cold sweat, afraid that I was about to lose everything I had worked so hard for. I'm sure you can relate to how I felt. Most of us operate under significant financial pressure and the stress that comes with it. Then one day I heard a teaching on Malachi 3:10 that changed by entire approach to the issue of finances: "'Bring the full tithe into the storehouse, so that there may be food in My house. Test Me in this,' says the LORD of Hosts. 'See if I will not open the windows of heaven and pour out for you blessing without measure.'"[36]

This scripture told me that to release my fear, I had to put my trust in the Creator of the universe as the source of my security, and that He would provide for me because *it is His nature to do so*. It was a hard decision at first to begin tithing ten percent of all my earnings, but this act of faith released the fear that had always held me back. And rather than feeling forced to tithe, I knew it was a matter of trusting that if I placed the whole issue of my finances into His hands, I could let fear go with it.

Nowhere has this been more apparent than when I made the decision to move to Kentucky. I was still drowning in debt at the time, but more doors opened than I could ever have predicted. I was able to sell my farm at my asking price and get out of debt,

Your New Beginning

and I landed a great job and was able to purchase land in Paris. Keep in mind that all this happened while I was practicing God's law of giving and receiving. It's been twelve years since I started tithing, and looking back, I can see that practicing generosity and trusting the Creator of the universe has opened the doors of abundance in my life, and released me from the captivity of fear. Along the way I have learned another crucial step to overcoming an attitude of lack, which is to consciously shift into a state of gratitude.

A HEART OF GRATITUDE
OPENS THE DOORS OF ABUNDANCE!

I've seen the power of these principles at work in others' lives as well. Remember the Crispell family I spoke of earlier, who lived on Abundant Life Farm? Encountering people that lived without any fear of lack was something completely new to me. They had a different perspective from anyone else I'd ever met because they believed God's universe was abundant, and they always demonstrated a heart of gratitude. Like most of us, at times they struggled financially and made mistakes, but they lived by an unshakeable faith that everything they needed would be provided for them. For example, at one point though finances were tight, they stepped out in faith and purchased a black Morgan yearling colt named Starbuck. He developed into a beautiful horse, and by his fourth year he won the New York State Fair Stallion Championship. A gentleman followed them back to his stall afterward, and said to Gloria, "I would love to buy your horse."

Without a second thought, she gave him the figure she knew would solve a lot of their financial problems: "We'd have to get a hundred thousand dollars to sell him." Much to her amazement, the gentleman accepted her price! Until then, the family had been struggling dairy farmers, but with the sale of Starbuck, they were quickly able to take themselves out of significant debt.

Even after that, God continued to supply them with resources, such as a gravel pit on their property, which they sold for a large amount of money. I was truly in awe of this family's faith and how their heart of gratitude always seemed to open the doors of abundance. Through the years, they expanded their farm to accommodate their growing extended family, and to continue offering hospitality to others as they had for me.

What I learned living on Abundant Life Farm is that when you combine doing what you love with hard work, generosity, and faith, the Creator will orchestrate events in His universe to provide every resource you need. My hope is that going forward, you can adopt a new perspective that the world is abundant in resources available to you, so you can have a heart of gratitude and live without fear of lack.

Action Step: A Heart of Gratitude

Write down one thing you can do to be more generous and practice gratitude, so you too can open the doors of abundance as you journey to your destination.

CHAPTER 5
Freedom Through Forgiveness

"Forgiveness does not change the past, but it does enlarge the future."[37]

—Paul Boese

To some extent, we all find ourselves captive at times to resentment. We can all relate to feeling disrespected or having someone fail our expectations, but it's the deep betrayals by people we trust and love, or who have power over us, that can linger for years. In order for you to expand your influence and live out your destiny, you're going to have to learn to work through unforgiveness and release yourself from toxic emotions that will rob you of the energy that's necessary to take this journey you're on. It can keep you up at night and steal the peace you need to live successfully and fulfill your dreams. I can't stress enough how important it is to let go of resentment *for your own sake*, so you can live fully into your purpose. St. Augustine's quote on the subject of forgiveness has been repeated so often that it's almost a cliché, but it's undeniably true: "Resentment is like drinking poison and waiting for the other person to die."

We are designed to thrive, and like seedlings, our dreams must be planted and nurtured in the proper environment to develop. You wouldn't plant a seed in toxic soil and expect it to thrive, but that's exactly what resentment is: TOXIC. So, how does one let go of resentment, especially when it's rooted in deep pain? Mary Morrissey's teachings on the nature and power of authentic forgiveness really helped me: "Forgiveness is… giving one perception for another."[38]

Forgiving is a process, and it can be a difficult one. You may need to begin by forgiving yourself—for hurting someone else or for past mistakes that you feel have permanently cost you your destiny. But, you must shift your perspective on the object of your resentment, even if it is you. Remember Chicken Man, whom you read about in Chapter 3? He's a perfect example of the cost of not forgiving oneself. Imagine if someone could have helped him change his perception toward himself as a human being who was the object of God's unconditional love. His life would have had a very different ending! Like him, we are all broken to some extent by shame or regret we can't seem to shake. But it's important to ask how not forgiving yourself for past mistakes is holding you back from living the life you desire. As much as we need to forgive others, we need to forgive ourselves, too.

I can relate to how hard Chicken Man was on himself. Waking up in a psychiatric hospital after my suicide attempt was not just a low, I felt I had veered completely off course regarding my life's vision. As a result of my past experiences, I felt totally lost and so jaded that I couldn't give myself a break. But, by committing daily to reject the self-punishment that wasn't serving my life's purpose, I could forgive myself and find my footing again. So, every morning, I purposely chose to see myself as a priceless creation separate from my past, because I knew that's how Jesus saw me. By replacing my flawed self-image for His perception of me, over time I was able to shift my paradigm, and negative feelings about my past no longer affected me the way they used to.

Therefore, if anyone is in Christ, he is a new creation. The old has passed away; behold, the new has come.

2 Corinthians 5:17 (ESV)

Action step: Forgiving Yourself

In your notebook, write down one mistake or situation that still causes you to feel regret today. It's critical to identify it so you can start shifting your perspective and forgive yourself for something that happened in the past. Forgiving yourself is necessary to finding freedom!

The Power of Compassion

Shifting from an attitude of resentment to one of compassion is a necessary step in your own healing process. Learning to see people who have wounded you as broken individuals with their own complicated stories will help you take their actions toward you less personally and free you from revisiting the pain and rehashing pointless self-dialogues around these offenses. This does not minimize or excuse what they've done, nor does it require that you expose yourself to their toxic behaviors again. What it does is free you from the containment of resentment so you can live out your destiny.

We can see the power of compassion to overcome deep betrayal in the life story of Joseph. His destiny was to establish and preserve the Israelites in the foreign land of Egypt long before their destiny to become a nation was fulfilled. When Joseph was a boy, God spoke to him through dreams, telling him he would someday rule over his brothers. Listen to one of the dreams that young Joseph shared with his family: "We were out in the field, tying up bundles of grain. Suddenly my bundle stood up, and your bundles all gathered around and bowed low before mine!" (Genesis 37:6-7 (NLT)).

It's easy to see how hearing this dream could provoke his older brothers' resentment. In addition, their father, Jacob, favored Joseph over the others and had given him a coat of many colors. This family dynamic caused the older siblings to hate him so much that they sold him into slavery in Egypt! Forced into servitude in the house of Potiphar, a prominent military leader, Joseph would suffer many trials, including false accusations of adultery by Potiphar's wife that resulted in his imprisonment.

Imagine finding yourself imprisoned in a foreign land through no fault of your own, heartbroken after being given such a strong vision for your life! I believe Joseph held these dreams close to his heart and in the forefront of his mind, and that they sustained him through these unimaginably harsh circumstances. While in captivity, he had the opportunity to interpret two of Pharaoh's dreams, one predicting a seven-year famine in Egypt:

> Behold, in my dream I was standing on the banks of the Nile. Seven cows, plump and attractive, came up out of the Nile and fed in the reed grass. Seven other cows came up after them, poor and very ugly and thin…the thin, ugly cows ate up the first seven plump cows…
>
> Genesis 41:17-20 (ESV)

Through his interpretation of Pharaoh's dream, Joseph was able to advise him to store up food for an upcoming famine. As a result, the ruler showed him favor and promoted him to the position of prime minister of Egypt! Now let's fast-forward two years to the famine devastating the land and surrounding nations. The people of Canaan were also running out of food, so Jacob sent his ten oldest sons to Egypt to buy goods:

> Now Joseph was the governor of the land, the person who sold grain to all its people. So when Joseph's brothers arrived, they bowed down to him with their faces to the ground. As soon as Joseph saw his brothers, he recognized them, but he pretended to be a stranger and spoke harshly to them. "Where do you come from?" he asked.
>
> Genesis 42:6-7 (NLT)

It would have been completely understandable if Joseph had given in to bitterness and used his position to take revenge on his brothers. But, he had experienced a shift in perspective, and he chose to extend compassion: "I *am* Joseph your brother, whom you sold into Egypt. But now, do not therefore be grieved or angry with yourselves because you sold me here; for God sent me before you to preserve life" (Genesis 45:5).

Joseph's response is a tremendous example of finding good in terrible circumstances. No one could have predicted that the brothers would stand before him one day, begging for food, fulfilling Joseph's dream of the bowing wheat bundles. Clearly, the Creator was orchestrating events all along. The seeds of the Promised Land were planted right there in Egypt, and Joseph became a founding father of the future nation of Israel.

We all can relate to feeling betrayed, but holding on to resentment will take your focus off of your vision and cost valuable energy you will need for your incredible journey. I encourage you, like Joseph, to choose compassion over revenge. Trusting God to use even the most difficult situation for your good frees *you* to advance into the unique purpose and vision He has for your life!

Action step: Shifting Your Perspective

Looking with compassion on people who have hurt you can be the key to freedom. Going forward, it's important that you look at the past from this new perspective. How can you apply this principle to a painful situation so you can be released from deep hurt and resentment?

Now, let's review the three key principles in this chapter that are necessary to break free from the toxic effects of resentment:

1. Identify the object of your resentment, whether it's yourself or someone else, so you can shift your perspective and GIVE one perception FOR another.

2. Remember that as a child of God, you have been forgiven. Choose to see yourself as a priceless creation separate from your past, because that is how He sees you.

3. Recognize that everyone has a complicated backstory. This shift in perspective allows you to show compassion towards someone who has deeply hurt you.

I want to end this chapter with the powerful words of C.S. Lewis: "To be a Christian means to forgive the inexcusable, because God has forgiven the inexcusable in you."

CHAPTER 6
Navigating by the Voice of Truth

Moses was a strong and courageous leader of the Israelites on their perilous journey from Egypt to the Promised Land. But more importantly, the Israelites had supernatural guidance directing their steps: "And the Lord went before them by day in a pillar of cloud, to lead them the way; and by night in a pillar of fire, to give them light; to go by day and night" (Exodus 13:21).

Now imagine you download an app on your cell phone called Life's Navigator, a built-in intelligence system you can refer to daily to keep you on track with your Promised Land vision. You get out of bed, eat and get dressed, and walk out your door where a cloud waits to guide you through your day. Then, as night falls, it switches to a pillar of fire to light your way through the darkness. This may sound like a science fiction movie, but the fact is that we have this application built into us. It's called God's Voice of Truth. In *Think and Grow Rich*, Napoleon Hill describes a phenomenon called Infinite Intelligence: "Infinite Intelligence is the force that gives order and origin to everything in the entire universe. It is the prime source, the first of everything that comes into existence."[39]

All the great transformational teachers believe in the concept of Infinite Intelligence, seeing it generally as a singular powerful source that operates the universe in perfect order. They believe connecting to this source is vital, in order to access the necessary information to operate at their highest genius level. As with the other ideas covered in this book, this is true because it is in perfect alignment with what the Creator of the universe tells us in His Word. This Infinite Intelligence was more than just a guide for the Israelites on their journey. It was present with them in the pillar of fire and cloud, and later dwelled with them even more intimately in the tabernacle God told them to build in the wilderness. This tent-like structure would be the place where He would speak with them directly. This is exciting news for you and me, because we, too, have direct communication with the one power and presence which operates the universe in perfect order. The Holy Spirit!

Intuition: The Still, Small Voice

Most of us navigate our way through life, taking in information through our five senses and using it to try to solve problems with our reasoning mind. This is what the world calls common sense, and it is how we are trained to respond to our environment. Don't get me wrong, this information is good insight to guide our decision-making, but there's more valuable information available to us through our intuition.

What exactly is intuition? It's the Voice of Truth, and it's like an additional sense that speaks to us from the day that we're born. This is very evident when watching small children operate instinctively in their intuition, before they begin developing harsh self-judgments and forming false paradigms. We need to familiarize ourselves with this internal voice again so we can begin operating more fully in our genius. Israel's prophet Elijah is a vivid example of getting in tune with this still, small Voice of Truth. He found himself hiding in a cave during a violent storm, fearing for his life as Queen Jezebel sought to assassinate him for killing the prophets of Baal. He was temporarily misdirected by fear, but he did the wise thing in responding to God's instruction to step out before Him in spite of the raging storm:

"Go out and stand on the mountain before the LORD. Behold, the LORD is about to pass by." And a great and mighty wind tore into the mountains and shattered the rocks before the LORD, but the LORD was not in the wind. After the wind there was an earthquake, but the LORD was not in the earthquake. After the earthquake came a fire, but the LORD was not in the fire. And after the fire came a still, small voice.[40]

1 Kings 19:11-13

Until that moment, Elijah had been relying on what he could see, hear, and feel in the natural world around him so that his focus was on his circumstances. You could say that he was trusting entirely in his human reasoning instead of listening for the still, small voice for the solution to his dilemma. By listening to God's direction, he was able to get his focus back on the true source of his power and security. We have this same intuition built into all of us as part of our birthright. The Creator's Infinite Intelligence is made known to us by His voice spoken through our intuition. This example illustrates our need to be directed by a power beyond our humanity, that can speak to the fears and worries of our current circumstances.

The lesson for us in Elijah's story is that we must shift our focus away from our storms so we can get quiet and hear the still, small Voice of Truth. I encourage you to set aside some time each day to get quiet and practice listening for His infinite Intelligence, which will provide the necessary information you need on your journey.

Edison: An Inventor's Intuition

Thomas Edison, best known for inventing the incandescent light bulb, had an unconventional method of getting quiet in order to receive critical information so he could find solutions to problems. He would sit in a chair with a steel ball in each hand. Under each hand he placed a steel plate. If he started to fall asleep, one of the balls would fall and the noise would wake him up so he could continue meditating on the solution for as long as it took to receive the answer: "My so-called inventions already existed in the environment. I've created nothing. Nobody does."[41]

Although Edison didn't say it directly, he believed in an Infinite Intelligence that held the solution to every problem. And, like Elijah, he had learned the value of removing himself from the intensity of the moment, and getting quiet so he could receive the answers he knew already existed in the universe. Elijah and Edison both learned to trust their intuition more than their five senses. Like your Promised Land vision, your intuition is a key component of your own Navigator app operating system. It's important to update this operating system daily by keeping your vision in the forefront of your mind. This will allow your intuition to increasingly guide your decisions. Your five senses will then begin to take on a secondary role in decision-making as you use your built-in navigation system on a daily basis and become accustomed to your new vision-based way of thinking.

Resourcefulness and Vision

Teddy Roosevelt was another powerful visionary thinker. His philosophy of Manifest Destiny, or personal and national expansion, has had a tremendous influence on America's cultural vision and history. A guiding principle of his life is captured in his famous quote: "Do what you can with what you have, where you are."[42] Just as Edison knew the answer to every problem already existed in Infinite Intelligence, Roosevelt knew that an infinite supply of resources were available and just waiting to be accessed. I have experienced this powerful truth myself. Remember the milk truck I spotted for sale on the side of the road, that later became my mobile blacksmithing service? This happened because I began looking at the world in a new vision-based way!

With the understanding that we live in a universe that's abundant in resources, going forward, you will start each day by asking the question, "What can I do with what I have available to me now, to get me one step closer to my Promised Land?" This will also train you to begin seeing possibilities around you that you may not have noticed before adopting your new vision-based way of observing the world.

> Ask and it will be given to you; seek and you will find;
> knock and the door will be opened to you.
>
> Matthew 7:7

A Critical Takeaway!

The most important takeaway from this chapter is that you are connected to God's Infinite Intelligence. This connection provides continual access to the necessary information to operate in a higher order of thinking, your genius. *Your genius is really your natural state and part of your birthright!* As you become more familiarized with the Voice of Truth through your intuition, you can move forward with a whole new level of confidence that every problem has a ready solution. *Remember there is always an answer!*

CHAPTER 7
Crossing the Jordan

"It is in your moments of decision that your destiny is shaped."[43]

—Tony Robbins

Now, it's time for you, like Joshua and Caleb, to make brave moves across the Jordan and advance confidently to your Promised Land. These two men entered the land of Canaan, confident they could scale the tall city walls and defeat the giants. Though they certainly experienced moments of failure, they kept their focus on their source of strength, and clung to His promise that they would inherit a land flowing with milk and honey. As you continue on your journey, you will face setbacks and failures, too, and your ability to move forward will depend on your perspective. A reporter once asked Thomas Edison, "How did it feel to fail 1,000 times?" Thomas's perspective on the idea of failure is critical to living one's dream: "I didn't fail 1,000 times. The light bulb was an invention with 1,000 steps."[44]

When you venture out into unfamiliar territory, you're going to experience setbacks, so it's important that you adopt a new perspective on failure as a steppingstone to a larger faith. Going back to Peter's story, it might look like he failed in his attempt to walk on water, but it was really the other disciples who chose the safety of the boat over stepping out in faith who really missed a learning opportunity.

We all experience failure and have been conditioned to see past mistakes as proof that our dream was a bad idea, not worth the risk, or someone else's destiny and not our own. I'm sure Peter felt this way after failing to walk on water, and maybe even embarrassed that he failed in front of the other disciples. I can imagine you have felt this way when you've made mistakes, too. I get it, welcome to the human race! But, failure is a necessary part of your journey! The idea is to view it as part of the learning process as you grow in your faith. Peter may have questioned his purpose as a leader after his moment of defeat, but as history shows, he didn't let his failures stop him and he grew into a strong and faithful leader.

Remember, I went through a very dark period where I felt like I had completely failed because I had tried to end my life. It was a very rough road for me for a lot of years. Not only did I hold my shame against myself for a long time, but I threw it back in my own face over and over again through negative self-dialogue. But once I discovered a new perspective on failure as part of life and necessary for growth, I made the conscious decision to stop punishing myself for not measuring up to the world's standards. As I reflect on my life's journey, I now see my failures as valuable experiences that have shaped me into who I am today. Going forward, I encourage you to welcome failure and see it as a stepping-stone to a larger faith.

Welcome failure? YES!

There's a well-known and surprising truth at the heart of the life-transformational movement: *Highly successful people have learned to welcome failure!* They have learned to use setbacks and moments of disappointment as feedback or necessary information to assess their progress and adjust their course. Price Pritchett explains this beautifully in his book *you*^{2}: "Unless you allow yourself to make mistakes, to fail, you will never have the opportunity to test the limits of what you truly are capable of accomplishing."[45]

Think of any highly successful person you admire. You will find that one thing they have in common with other successful people is a total commitment to their vision and purpose in life. They respond to setbacks and adapt, but they never give up! Remember, Penny Chenery was deeply in debt and under a lot of pressure to sell Secretariat, but she never wavered in her strong commitment to making him a champion racehorse to honor her father's legacy. Like Penny, you will need to decide to commit to your dream, even while knowing that you'll experience failure at times. This is the point where many people choose to give up on their dream—they focus on their circumstances and give in to the temptation to return back to the "Egypt mindset" and they remain captive to the past. But going forward, you will see failure as a chance to test your limits and show you what you're capable of.

If you give in to anything, give in to a new habit of not giving up. This new habit, like a muscle, will need to be exercised repeatedly so it becomes stronger and using it becomes second nature to you. Then you will develop the endurance to press on whenever feelings of discouragement tempt you to look backward instead of forward.

Having the correct perspective on failure is liberating, especially in those moments you feel tempted to give up on your dream. It is important at such moments to ask the Creator, "Is this the path I should be on, or do you have something better in mind for me?" He will show you if you are on the right course or not, by either increasing your enthusiasm to keep going or by redirecting your path. Adopting the approach of, "This or something greater, God," removes the power of discouragement to influence what you do next. Adjusting one's course is fine, giving up is not.

Action Step: Forward After Failure

In your notebook, write down a past failure that has left you feeling defeated and keeps you from advancing toward your dreams. How can you shift your perspective and see this failure as valuable information to get you back on course instead?

Cultivating Greatness

Like me, Thomas Edison had a mother who spoke positive words over her son, and cultivated greatness in him:

One day Thomas Edison came home and gave a paper to his mother. He told her, "My teacher gave this paper to me and told me to only give it to my mother."

His mother's eyes were tearful as she read the letter out loud to her child: *Your son is a genius. This school is too small for him and doesn't have enough good teachers for training him. Please teach him yourself.*

Many years later, after Edison's mother died and he had become one of the greatest inventors of the century, one day he was looking through old family things. Suddenly he saw a folded paper in the corner of a drawer in a desk. He took it and opened it up. On the paper was written: *Your son is addled* [mentally ill]. *We won't let him come to school anymore.*[46]

Edison cried for hours and then he wrote in his diary: "Thomas Alva Edison was an addled child that, by a hero mother, became the genius of the century."[47]

Secretariat also possessed greatness, and Penny nurtured it until he was able to live out his destiny to become a legend. Moses, Joshua, and Caleb also possessed greatness, and from the moment they led the Israelites out of Egypt and through the Red Sea, they never stopped running toward the land and freedom that was promised to them. But first, God had to replace the Israelites' false identity as slaves with a new vision to keep them moving forward into their purpose as His chosen people, and their destiny to establish a new nation. Throughout their journey, they learned to put fear and doubt behind them and form a whole new perspective based on His abundance and provision. They overcame bitterness and received forgiveness and developed a deeper relationship with the Creator. This new intimacy with Him allowed them to hear the Voice of Truth directly and receive the necessary information to keep them on course toward the Jordan River. Even after Moses learned that his striking of the rock in anger would keep him from entering into the Promised Land, he chose to cultivate greatness. Rather than focus on feelings of failure, he chose instead to impart a blessing to those who would go on to establish the nation of Israel:

> I place before you Life and Death, Blessing and Curse. Choose life so that you and your children will live. And love God, your God, listening obediently to him, firmly embracing him. Oh yes, he is life itself, a long life settled on the soil that God, your God, promised to give your ancestors, Abraham, Isaac, and Jacob.
>
> Deuteronomy 30:15 (The Message)

Here, Moses is a living example of how we are to respond to disappointment and failure—he speaks life over others, and so should we. Speaking life into setbacks allows us to cultivate greatness out of every circumstance.

After Moses' death, under Joshua and Caleb's leadership the Israelites never retreated, learning from each failure as they advanced toward the Promised Land. We can see through their forty-year wilderness experience that God used this time to cultivate in them a bigger belief in what was possible with Him, so that by the time they reached the walls of Jericho, they were ready to obey His voice and achieve victories the world would have called impossible.

Like them, you have a birthright and a unique purpose, and now you possess the necessary weapons to slay any giants that stand in your way as you navigate to your Promised Land. Regardless of what triumphs and failures have brought you to this point, today is your divine appointment—Your New Beginning—and with the principles taught in this book, you've acquired a new set of tools you can apply going forward on your own heroic journey. And hopefully, now you have come to see yourself in the Israelites' story and have begun to adopt a Joshua and Caleb mindset that's ready to claim your Promised Land vision today. The seeds of greatness exist within you, and you're cultivating a bigger belief in what's possible as you walk daily with the Creator of the universe. As His child, you are destined for greater things than you ever imagined.

> I tell you the truth, anyone who believes in me will do the same works I have done, and even greater works...
>
> John 14:12 (NLT)

CHAPTER 8
Joy in the Journey

"Happiness is the ability to move forward knowing the future will be better than the past."[48]

—Zig Ziglar

My Promised Land journey started the day I graduated from high school, in a conversation with my good friend Marcia. After the ceremony, she hugged me and told me that she believed I would be successful at any endeavor I chose in life. Her words stuck with me as I walked away, and I told myself that someday I would live on my own horse farm in Kentucky and would be a successful motivational speaker and teacher. These were more than just ambitions, they were dreams deeply embedded in my heart, that gave me life and were truly what I wanted to become.

Likewise, it's important that your purpose and dream are both deeply rooted in something that brings you life and that you genuinely love doing. On a recent visit to a horse farm, I was drawn to a beautiful chestnut yearling colt with a proud stature and the most striking eyes. I asked about his breeding and if he was for sale. He was, and amazingly his pedigree traced back to Will Shriver and Sultan's Santana, the two horses mentioned earlier in this book who inspired my journey! I had the opportunity to purchase him, and to honor his proud history I named him Will Bennett after his grandsire Will Shriver and his breeder Dr. Scott Bennett, the famous Kentucky equine veterinarian.

I see Will as a gift from God, and the perfect representation of how a continuous commitment to one's vision can bring our dreams to fruition.

I'm excited for the next stage of my Promised Land journey with Will, which is to compete at the famous Lexington Junior League Horse Show and then to win the world title in harness driving at the Kentucky State Fair. While I work towards achieving these important goals as a horseman, my highest purpose and passion remains to encourage others to live out the life God intends for them. It is my hope that as you advance toward your Promised Land, that you find joy in your journey as I have, and in the process come to truly grasp your infinite worth.

The completion of this book represents a pinnacle for me, being exactly forty years from the birth of my dream on high school graduation day. And I don't believe it's a coincidence that like the Israelites' journey to the Promised Land, my own has taken forty years. As God was present and guided them through the wilderness, He has been with me on my journey and will also be with you: "As I was with Moses, so I will be with you; I will never leave you nor forsake you. Be strong and courageous..." (Joshua 1:5-6 (Berean Study Bible).

I hope you recognize after reading this book that you, too, are connected to the one power and presence that operates the universe in perfect order. When I look back and see all the ways the Creator has orchestrated events for my success, I recognize that His truth is at the heart of Thoreau's statement: "If one advances confidently in the direction of his dreams, and endeavors to live the life which he has imagined, he will meet with a success unexpected in common hours."[49]

I was no more destined for greatness when I started my journey than you are. The principles in this book are for anyone who is willing to apply them to his or her life. All I did was claim my destiny and start applying them myself, which enabled me to interrupt the old paradigms that had once kept me circling in the wilderness.

This set me free to run after my destiny with a vision-based way of thinking, what I call a "Joshua and Caleb mindset."

By developing this powerful mindset and putting these principles into practice yourself, your own journey does not have to take forty years. Penny Chenery is another great example of how these principles can work in service of one's purpose. Through commitment, determination and strong belief in her dream, she helped make Secretariat Time Magazine's Super Horse[50] of all time and became the first woman to successfully establish herself in the male-dominated world of horse racing. I'm going to encourage you, like Penny and Secretariat, to keep running until you reach your destination. Make the decision today to move confidently in the direction of your dreams with your vision in front of you, knowing that you don't travel alone. The Creator of the Universe will be your compass and guiding light every step of the way. Whatever challenges or problems arise, He will orchestrate your steps and faithfully provide the answers you need.

Thy Word is a lamp to my feet and a light to my path.

Psalm 119:105 (NASB)

1973 Triple Crown Winner Secretariat Time magazine

Your New Beginning

Penny Chenery and her beloved horse Secretariat

Secretariat running with all 4 hoofs off the ground

Your New Beginning

1976 World Champion Will Shriver
and his trainer Redd Crabtree

Chapter 8

My Kentucky home and horse barn

My beloved horse Will Bennett

Frank Garguilo and Will Bennett

A FINAL THOUGHT: BROADCASTING BELIEF

In the 1950s, Earl Nightingale became one of the first people to broadcast a radio show about the life-transformational principles that are still taught today. This brief excerpt from one of his broadcasts reveals the key to success or failure: "Throughout all history the great wise men and teachers, philosophers… disagreed with one another on many different things. It is only on this one point that they are in complete and unanimous agreement. WE BECOME WHAT WE THINK ABOUT."[51]

This foundational truth—that we *become* what we think about—originates in the Word of God and is stated perfectly in Proverbs 23:7 (NKJV): "…as a man thinketh in his heart, so is he."

This truth was the inspiration for the Concord Conversations and the Transcendentalist movement led by Ralph Waldo Emerson and was affirmed by Henry David Thoreau's experiment on Walden Pond. Their writings influenced authors like Napoleon Hill, whose classic book *Think and Grow Rich* has been read by generations desiring to build lives of purpose. But as you journey forward as a child of God, grounded in His Word and guided by the Holy Spirit, this truth will take on even deeper meaning as you pursue your destiny, and a life of purpose *and* joy.

"Your purpose and a joyful life are intimately connected."[52]

—Mary Crockford

7 Steps to Crossing the Jordan:

1. Read your purpose, vision statement, and affirmations each day and night. This will help you to begin imagining yourself living in the Promised Land.
2. Keep advancing confidently toward your dreams and make the decision daily that *nothing* is going to stop you from reaching your destination. Remember, you are far greater than your circumstances!
3. Continue to shift your perspective daily as you work through your false paradigms so that emotions of fear, worry, and unforgiveness no longer have their old power over you.
4. Familiarize yourself with the Voice of Truth through your own intuition so that you can receive the information you need to reach your destination.
5. Ask the question daily: "What can I do with what I have available to me now, to get me one step closer to the Promised Land?" Once you receive the answer you need from God's Infinite Intelligence, proceed with an action step!
6. Use any failures you may experience as feedback so you can adjust your course when necessary.
7. DON'T FORGET TO FIND JOY IN YOUR JOURNEY!

A Promised Land Prayer for You

I pray that you will step out boldly, knowing that as God's highest form of creation, you have great value and a unique purpose on this Earth. I pray you discover that purpose and a vision that serves it, and that you are set free from every false paradigm that has held you captive so you can co-create the joyful and abundant life He intends for you. As you journey out of the familiar into new territory in pursuit of your dreams, my hope is that you grow in faith and confidence with each step. And like Moses, Joshua and Caleb, I pray you speak life over yourself and others, and inspire them to enter the Promised Land with you. I leave you with the words of Deuteronomy 31:8 (NKJV), which God spoke to Joshua at the moment the Israelites entered into the Promised Land: "And the Lord, He is the One who goes before you. He will be with you, He will not leave you nor forsake you; do not fear nor be dismayed."

Live your dream to His Glory. Amen!

AFTERWORD

At the start of my Promised Land journey, I was so intrigued by Thoreau's experiment that I wanted to do my own condensed version of it based on Jeremiah 29:11: "'For I know the plans I have for you,' declares the Lord, 'plans to prosper you and not to harm you, plans to give you hope and a future.'" So, for seven months, I reminded myself of this verse every morning and trusted that God would bless my endeavors and provide the resources needed to take this journey. At first, I was full of hope; however, halfway into the experiment, I returned to my old condition-based way of thinking, and I became overwhelmed with the fear of failure. So, one morning, I asked the Holy Spirit for His help to relieve my anxiety. At first, I didn't receive an answer; however, later that day while doing my barn chores, I heard God's voice clearly say to me, "Frank I am your security." This was life changing, and it gave me the confidence to keep moving forward in the direction of my dreams. At the end of my experiment, I had only made a few steps towards my destination. However, I developed a stronger faith watching how He provided for me. I continued my journey through the wilderness and overcame my unhealthy paradigms by daily applying the new Joshua and Caleb mindset, along with trusting in the promise found in Jeremiah 29:11. Forty months later I successfully reached my Promised Land.

I am so grateful for God's sovereignty and conclude with, "If you entrust your Life and dreams to Jesus Christ, He will provide the wisdom and resources needed for your success."

BIBLIOGRAPHY

Berean Study Bible, Berean Bible, 2020, Bible Hub, biblehub.com/bsb/.

Boese, Paul. Weekly Digest, 19 Feb. 1967.

Brown, Les. "The Story of Chicken Man." *YouTube*, 6 May 2015, youtube.com/watch?v=4IKD8k0QRBA.

"But They Did Not Give Up." Self-Efficacy Site, University of Kentucky, 21 Aug. 2000, uky.edu/~eushe2/Pajares/OnFailingG.html.

Campbell, Ernest T. "Sermon: Give Ye Them to Eat. The Riverside Church," 1970, Internet Archive, archive.org/details/sermongiveyethem00camp/mode/2up.

Canfield, Jack. *The Success Principles*. Edited by Janet Switzer, 10th Anniversary Edition ed., William Morrow, 2007.

Chiavaroli, Heidi. "The Beautiful Renewal of Forgiving When It's Hard." *Crosswalk.com*, Salem Web Network, 12 Feb. 2021, crosswalk.com/faith/spiritual-life/the-beautiful-renewal-of-forgiving-when-its-hard.html.

Choong, Kevin. "6 Great Lessons You Can Learn from Theodore Roosevelt." *Addicted 2 Success*, 25 Mar. 2015, addicted2success.com/quotes/6-great-lessons-you-can-learn-from-theodore-roosevelt/.

Crockford, Mary. *Discovering Joy in the Journey.* Interview with Frank Garguilo, 8 October 2021. Paris, Kentucky.

"Edison, The Genius of the Century." Learn to Be Motivated, Blogspot, 25 Apr. 2019, learntobemotivated.blogspot. com/2019/04/thomas-alva-edison.html. Accessed 24 Jan. 2022.

Gray, Gordon, Mark Ciardi et. al. Secretariat. Walt Disney Studios Motion Pictures, 2010.

Gentry, Tony. Jesse Owens: Champion Athlete (Black Americans of Achievement). Hardcover. Chelsea House Publications, 2005.

Haden, Jeff. "100 Years Ago, Thomas Edison Perfectly Described the Difference between Successful Innovators and Those Who Only Dream." Inc., Mansueto Venture, 5 Dec. 2019.

Hill, Napoleon. Think and Grow Rich. Ralston Society, 1937.

Holy Bible, Contemporary English Version, American Bible Society, 2006, Bible Hub, biblehub.com/cev/.

Holy Bible, English Standard Version., Good News Publishers, 2001, Bible Hub, biblehub.com/esv/.

Holy Bible, King James Version. Bible Hub, biblehub.com/kjv/.

Holy Bible, New American Standard Bible., Good News Publishers, 2001, Bible Hub, biblehub.com/nasb/.

Holy Bible, New King James Version. Thomas Nelson, 1982, Bible Hub, biblehub.com/nkjv/.

Holy Bible, New Living Translation. Tyndale House Foundation, 2015, Bible Hub, biblehub.com/nlt/.

Kasprak, Alex. "Did Thomas Edison's Mother Lie About a Letter Expelling Him from School?" Snopes, 2016, https://www.snopes.com/fact-check/thomas-edisons-mom-lied-about-a-letter-expelling-her-son-from-school/#:~:-text=Many%20years%20after%20Edison%27s%20

mother%20had%20died%2C%20he,We%20cannot%20
let%20him%20attend%20our%20school%20anymore.

King, Jr., Martin Luther. "Martin Luther King's Speech: 'I
Have A Dream'—The Full Text." ABC News. March on
Washington, 23 Aug. 1963, Washington, D.C.,abcnews.
go.com/Politics/martin-luther-kings-speech-dream-full-
text/story?id=14358231.

Maltz, Maxwell. "General Principles." Psycho-Cybernetics,
Deluxe Edition ed., TarcherPerigree, 2016, p. x.

Morrissey, Mary. "5 Ways to Position Your Life for Greater
Abundance." Brave Thinking Institute, 12 Sept. 2019,
bravethinkinginstitute.com/blog/life-transformation/at-
tracting-abundance.

Morrissey, Mary. "Are You Drinking Poison, and Expecting the
Other Person to Die?" Brave Thinking Institute, 23 Mar.
2020, bravethinkinginstitute.com/blog/life-transforma-
tion/letting-go-of-resentment.

Morrissey, Mary. DreamBuilder Program. Brave Thinking Institute, Life SOULutions That Work, LLC, 2016. (Mem-
ber access only.)

Morrissey, Mary. "Evocative Coaching." Certified DreamBuilder Life Coaching Series. Mar. 2019, Los Angeles, Los
Angeles Airport Marriott.

Nightingale, Earl. "The Strangest Secret ." YouTube, 22 June
2019, youtube.com/watch?v=F4s1Fyh4HAg.

Peterson, Eugene H. The Message. NavPress, 2018, Bible Gate-
way, biblegateway.com/versions/Message-MSG-Bible/.

Peterson, Lindsay. "How I Found My Purpose." Words by L.
Peterson, 12 Jan. 2022. wordsbylpeterson.com/words/
howifoundmypurpose. Accessed 9 Sept. 2020.

Pritchett, Price. You²: A High-Velocity Formula for Multiplying Your Personal Effectiveness in Quantum Leaps. Rep Edition ed., Pritchett LP, 2012.

Proctor, Bob. "A Legitimate Mind Trick for Earning More Money." Proctor Gallagher Institute, 2 Aug. 2018, proctorgallagherinstitute.com/6880/a-legitimate-mind-trick-for-earning-more-money.

Proctor, Bob. Decision. PDF, dplocjsv6edhk.cloudfront.net/marketing/Decision%20by%20Bob%20Proctor.pdf.

Robbins, Tony. "20 Inspirational Quotes that Will Help You Achieve Success." Tony Robbins, Robbins Research International, Inc., tonyrobbins.com/tony-robbins-quotes/inspirational-quotes/.

Say, Jeremiah. "101 Zig Ziglar Quotes on Fear & Goals (MOTIVATION)." Gracious Quotes, 4 Feb. 2021, graciousquotes.com/zig-ziglar/.

Shaw, George Bernard. Mrs. Warren's Profession. PDF, 1893, Project Gutenberg, gutenberg.org/files/1097/1097-h/1097-h.htm.

Thoreau, Henry David. Walden & On the Duty of Civil Disobedience. Ticknor and Fields, 1862, Full Text Archive, fulltextarchive.com/pdfs/Walden-by-Henry-David-Thoreau.pdf.

Time Magazine. "Super Horse Secretariat." 1 Jan. 1973.

Wayne, John. "John Wayne Quotes." Goodreads, Goodreads Inc., goodreads.com/quotes/13533-courage-is-being-scared-to-death-but-saddling-up-anyway.

"XI. Immortality." The Complete Works of Ralph Waldo Emerson, by Ralph Waldo Emerson and Edward W. Emerson, Houghton, Mifflin, 1904, bartleby.com/90/0811.html.

ENDNOTES

1 John 14:12, *Holy Bible, New International Version.*

2 *Walden,* 362.

3 *The Complete Works of Ralph Waldo Emerson,* 1904.

4 Time Magazine, 1 Jan. 1973.

5 Walt Disney Studios, 2010.

6 *Success Principles* 23.

7 Morrissey, "Evocative Coaching," 2019.

8 *Walden,* 362.

9 *Sermon: Give ye them to eat,* 8.

10 Peterson, L. 2022.

11 Quoted by Say, "101 Quotes."

12 *Holy Bible, King James Version.*

13 Full transcript, ABC News 2013.

14 *Holy Bible, New Living Translation.*

15 Quotes by Gentry 2005.

16 Walt Disney Studios, 2010.

17 *Decision,* 1970.

18 *Walden,* 362.

19 *It's Not About the Money,* Chapter 6.

20 Shaw, *Mrs. Warren's Profession.*

21 "The Story of Chicken Man," *YouTube,* 2015.

22 *Psycho-Cybernetics,* Preface, *x.*

23 *Think and Grow Rich,* 95-96.

24 Quoted by Proctor, "A Legitimate Mind Trick for Earning More Money."

25 Morrissey, *Dream*builder Program.

26 Pritchett, 16.

27 Pritchett, 15.

28 Pritchett, 16.

29 Morrissey, *Dream*builder Program.

30 *Holy Bible, New King James Version, et al.*

31 Matthew 16:23, *Holy Bible, New International Version.*

32 Peterson, *The Message.*

33 *Holy Bible, New International Version.* Author brackets.

34 "John Wayne Quotes." *Goodreads.*

35 Robbins, Tony. "20 INSPIRATIONAL QUOTES."

36 *Berean Study Bible.*

37 Quoted in *Weekly Digest* 53:8, 146.

38 Morrissey, *Dream*builder Program. Author emphasis added.

39 *Holy Bible, King James Version.*

40 *Berean Study Bible.*

41 Quoted by Haden, "100 Years Ago."

42 Quoted by Choong, "6 Great Lessons."

43 Robbins, Tony. "20 INSPIRATIONAL QUOTES.*"*

44 Quoted in "But They Did Not Give Up."

45 Pritchett, 25.

46 https://www.snopes.com/fact-check/thomas-edisons-mom-lied-about-a-letter-expelling-her-son-from-school/#:~:text=Many%20years%20after%20Edison%27s%20mother%20had%20died%2C%20he,We%20cannot%20let%20him%20attend%20our%20school%20anymore.

47 "Edison, the Genius of the Century."

48 Quoted by Say, GraciousQuotes.com.

49 *Walden*, 362.

50 Time Magazine, 1 Jan. 1973.

51 "The Greatest Secret," *YouTube* 2019.

52 Crockford, *Discovering Joy in the Journey*, 2021.

Milton Keynes UK
Ingram Content Group UK Ltd.
UKHW020735271123
433342UK00009B/74